Slithering Snakes

King Cobras

by Suzane Nguyen

Blastoff! Readers 2

BELLWETHER MEDIA • MINNEAPOLIS, MN

Blastoff! Readers are carefully developed by literacy experts to build reading stamina and move students toward fluency by combining standards-based content with developmentally appropriate text.

Level 1 provides the most support through repetition of high-frequency words, light text, predictable sentence patterns, and strong visual support.

Level 2 offers early readers a bit more challenge through varied sentences, increased text load, and text-supportive special features.

Level 3 advances early-fluent readers toward fluency through increased text load, less reliance on photos, advancing concepts, longer sentences, and more complex special features.

★ **Blastoff! Universe**

This edition first published in 2025 by Bellwether Media, Inc.

Library of Congress Cataloging-in-Publication Data

Names: Nguyen, Suzane, author.
Title: King cobras / by Suzane Nguyen.
Description: Minneapolis, MN : Bellwether Media, Inc., 2025. | Series: Blastoff! readers: slithering snakes | Includes bibliographical references and index. | Audience: Ages 5-8 | Audience: Grades K-1 | Summary: "Simple text and full-color photography introduce beginning readers to king cobras. Developed by literacy experts for students in kindergarten through third grade"-- Provided by publisher.
Identifiers: LCCN 2024003107 (print) | LCCN 2024003108 (ebook) | ISBN 9798886870404 (library binding) | ISBN 9781644878842 (ebook)
Subjects: LCSH: King cobra--Juvenile literature. | Cobras--Juvenile literature.
Classification: LCC QL666.O64 N48 2025 (print) | LCC QL666.O64 (ebook) | DDC 597.96/42--dc23/eng/20240208
LC record available at https://lccn.loc.gov/2024003107
LC ebook record available at https://lccn.loc.gov/2024003108

Editor: Betsy Rathburn Designer: Brittany McIntosh

Printed in the United States of America, North Mankato, MN.

Table of Contents

King of Snakes

King cobras are dangerous snakes. Their **venom** can take down an elephant!

They live in India, China, and throughout Southeast Asia.

King Cobra Range

King cobras can have black, green, brown, or yellow **scales**. They have sharp **fangs**.

The **hoods** on their necks can open wide!

Spot a King Cobra!

King cobras are the world's longest venomous snakes. They grow up to 18 feet (5.5 meters) long!

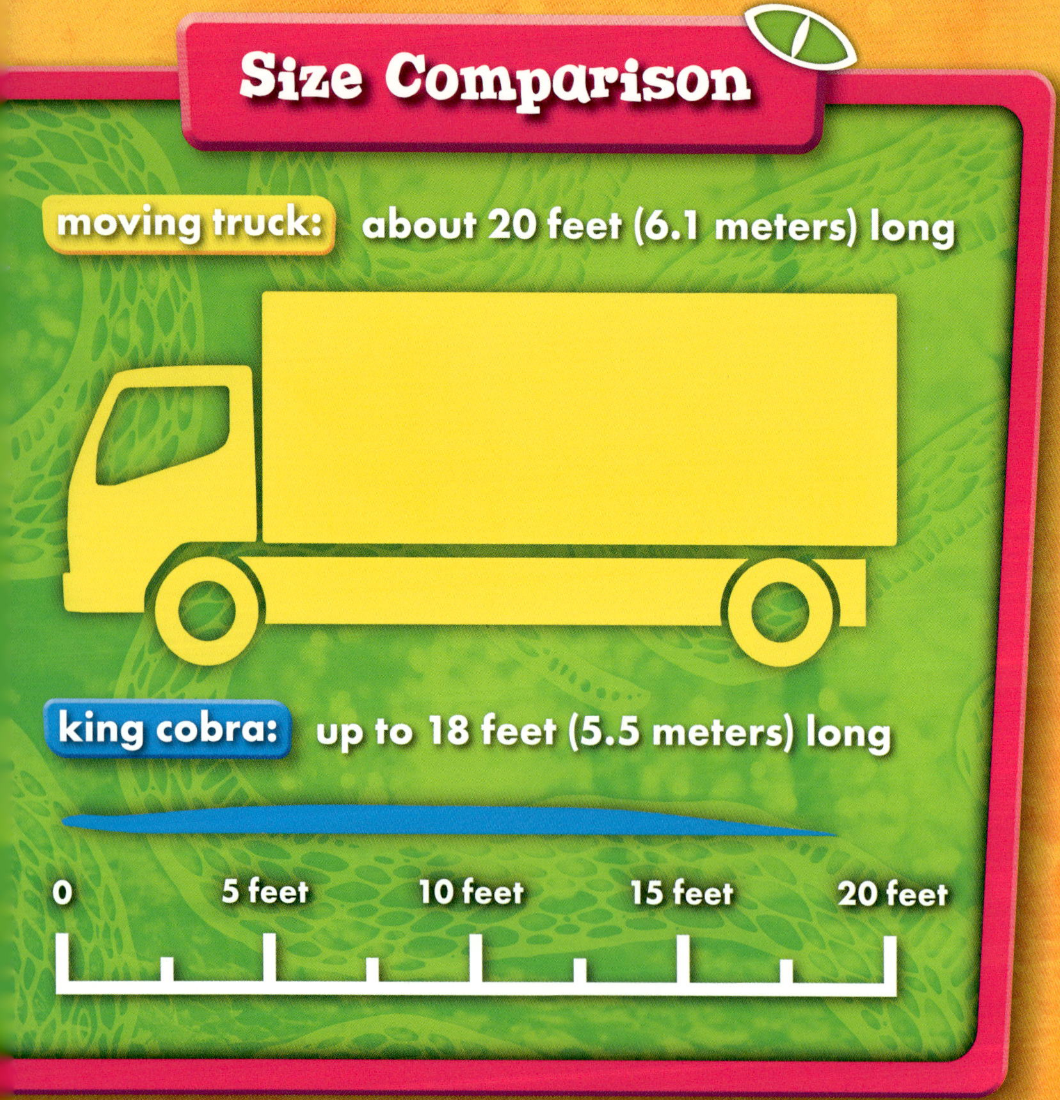

They weigh up to 20 pounds (9.1 kilograms).

Snake Eaters

King cobras mostly live in **rain forests**. They spend much of their time in trees or bushes.

They also live in **swamps** and **grasslands**.

King cobras are most active during the day. Their **forked** tongues smell for **prey**.

They mostly eat other snakes. They sometimes eat lizards and small **mammals**.

King Cobra Food

snakes

lizards

small mammals

When king cobras spot their meal, they bite! Venom from their fangs **stuns** prey.

Their fangs face backwards. This helps push prey down their throats.

King cobras have few **predators**. But mongooses hunt them.

mongoose

The cobras raise themselves up to scare enemies. They hiss and open their hoods!

On Their Own

King cobras are the only snakes that make nests. Females lay up to 40 eggs in the nest.

They attack anything
that comes near!

Baby king cobras can hunt right after they are born. They are adults after around five years.

Then they can make nests of their own!

King Cobra Stats

status in the wild: vulnerable

life span: around 20 years

Glossary

fangs—long, sharp teeth

forked—split into two parts

grasslands—lands covered with grasses and other soft plants with few bushes or trees

hoods—parts on the necks of some snakes that are used to scare away predators

mammals—warm-blooded animals that have backbones and feed their young milk

predators—animals that hunt other animals for food

prey—animals that are hunted by other animals for food

rain forests—thick, green forests that receive a lot of rain

scales—plates that cover an animal's body

stuns—makes motionless

swamps—wetlands filled with trees and other woody plants

venom—poison produced by an animal, usually for hunting

To Learn More

AT THE LIBRARY

Feldman, Thea. *Snakes Smell with Their Tongues!: And Other Amazing Facts.* New York, N.Y.: Simon Spotlight, 2021.

Jaycox, Jaclyn. *King Cobras.* Mankato, Minn.: Pebble Books, 2023.

Pallotta, Jerry. *Ultimate Reptile Rumble.* New York, N.Y.: Scholastic Inc., 2021.

ON THE WEB

FACTSURFER

Factsurfer.com gives you a safe, fun way to find more information.

1. Go to www.factsurfer.com.
2. Enter "king cobras" into the search box and click 🔍.
3. Select your book cover to see a list of related content.

Index

The images in this book are reproduced through the courtesy of: reptiles4all, front cover, p. 7; Eric Isselee, pp. 3, 23; Biju/ Alamy, p. 4; Michael Fitzsimmons/ Alamy, p. 6; DSlight_photography, pp. 9, 17; SuperStock/ Daniel Heuclin/ Biosphoto, pp. 10, 14, 20; Jan Bartonik, p. 11; SuperStock/ Malcolm Schuyl/ Frank Lane Picture Agency, p. 12; Lucas Mello/ Alamy, pp. 12-13; Prajjwal Ray, p. 13 (snakes); MWFP84, p. 13 (lizards); Nigel Dowsett, p. 13 (small mammals); Malcolm Schuyl/ Alamy, pp. 15, 18; Supriyo Ghoshal, p. 16; Jim Lambert, p. 19; Dezay, pp. 20-21.

Library Technology
R E P O R T S

Expert Guides to Library Systems and Services

Data Visualization with R for Digital Collections

Monika Glowacka-Musial

ALA TechSource
alatechsource.org

American Library Association

Library Technology
REPORTS

ALA TechSource purchases fund advocacy, awareness, and accreditation programs for library professionals worldwide.

Volume 57, Number 1
Data Visualization with R for Digital Collections
ISBN: 978-0-8389-4821-7
DOI: https://doi.org/10.5860/ltr.57n1

American Library Association
225 N. Michigan Ave., Suite 1300
Chicago, IL 60601-7616 USA
alatechsource.org
800-545-2433, ext. 4299
312-944-6780
312-280-5275 (fax)

Advertising Representative
Patrick Hogan
phogan@ala.org
312-280-3240

Editor
Patrick Hogan
phogan@ala.org
312-280-3240

Copy Editor
Judith Lauber

Production
ALA Production Services

Cover Design
Alejandra Diaz and ALA Production Services

Library Technology Reports (ISSN 0024-2586) is published eight times a year (January, March, April, June, July, September, October, and December) by American Library Association, 225 N. Michigan Ave., Suite 1300, Chicago, IL 60601-7616. It is managed by ALA TechSource, a unit of the publishing department of ALA. Periodical postage paid at Chicago, Illinois, and at additional mailing offices. POSTMASTER: Send address changes to Library Technology Reports, 225 N. Michigan Ave., Suite 1300, Chicago, IL 60601-7616.

ALA TechSource
alatechsource.org

About the Author

Monika Glowacka-Musial is a metadata librarian at New Mexico State University Library. She earned an MA in Polish literature and language from the University of Warsaw, Poland, a PhD in anthropology from Temple University, and an MA in library and information science from the University of Arizona. She also received a certificate in digital information management from the University of Arizona. One important aspect of her current position is exploring ways in which digital content can be enriched, shared, and engaged with creatively. She has taken several courses in coding, including Python and R, and she has found R especially manageable for noncoders and applicable to data visualization.

Abstract

Since the 1990s, libraries have invested in developing digital collections and online services to provide access to historical sources. One way to inspire users to actively engage with these materials is by creating visual contexts for the materials. These visuals provide an overview of a collection's content and inspire users to experiment with the collection's data for various purposes, including research.

This issue of *Library Technology Reports* (vol. 57, no. 1) presents an approach that views digital collections as data that can be mined, analyzed, and visualized by means of the R programming language. R is open source, relatively easy to learn, and supported by an established community of coders. The selection of plots presented in the report includes R scripts, fragments of data tables, and some explanation of the R code used to create the plots.

Subscriptions

alatechsource.org/subscribe